DOWNLOAD

THE LOWDOWN What? How? Who?

POLLY BIRKBECK AND NICOLA SLADE

DOWNLOAD

THE LOWDOWN What? How? Who?

POLLY BIRKBECK AND NICOLA SLADE

First published in Great Britain in 2006 by Virgin Books Ltd
Virgin Books Ltd
Thames Wharf Studios
Rainville Road
London
W6 9HA

A catalogue record for this book is available from the British Library.

ISBN-10 0 7535 1168 1
ISBN-13 9 780 7535 1168 8

The paper used in this book is a natural, recyclable product made from wood
grown in sustainable forests. The manufacturing process conforms to the regu-
lations of the country of origin.

Designed and typeset by Virgin Books Ltd
Printed and bound in Great Britain by The Bath Press

CONTENTS

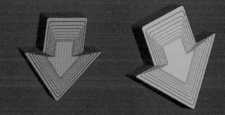

INTRODUCTION

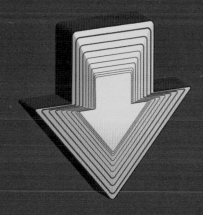

The digital world is a fast changing one, so quick that it's difficult to keep tabs on what it all means and, more importantly, what it can offer you. Within the last seven years, downloading has come up from the underground – the illegal file sharing of the Napster Version One era – to the mainstream in the form of iTunes and the phenomenon of the iPod.

During that time it's been hard to escape technology's growth and its grip on a whole new breed of people who are using their computers to do a lot more than send an email, check some flight prices, write a document or put together a spreadsheet for the family accounts.

The proliferation of the market and its sheer scale has done anything but make it easier. Tap in 'music downloading' or 'digital playlists' into a search engine and you're going to be hit with millions upon millions of search results, some of which will be of no use to you whatsoever.

This is a guide to help you cut through the useless search results and provide you with some tangible, understandable information, whether you are stepping on to the digital carousel for the first time, or would simply like to learn a little bit more about what is really possible.

We will scoot through various topics, beginning with downloading music to portable devices and which devices are out there – from digital audio players and personal media players through to mobile phones. We will talk you through the different services available for downloading, from online download stores to the download offerings that have been put in place by the mobile phone companies. We will explain some of those technical terms and acronyms that fluster the best of us and will briefly look at some future developments bound to shape the way you acquire your digital music collection. Finally, you'll find a small dictionary explaining some of the technical terms and products explained in the next few chapters.

So, it's time to look at that tired CD collection and discover the ways you can invigorate your library. First things first: you're going to need a digital music player!

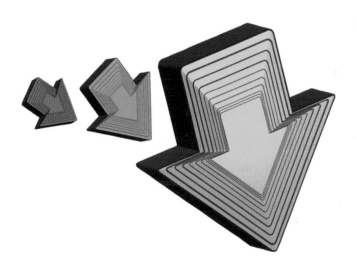

DIGITAL AUDIO DEVICES

The image of the dancing silhouette wearing white headphones has been on every billboard, TV screen, tube poster, magazine and newspaper, and unless you've been living on a desert island (with your old-fashioned discs!), it's been impossible to get away from Apple's advertising campaign. Surely now we all know what an iPod is?

Apple's marketing – even if it didn't make you rush out and buy an iPod – brought the 'digital revolution' in front of everyone's eyes, so much so that now we all know what an MP3 player is.

Apple's sleek machine isn't the only digital device on the market though; there's a whole variety of digital audio devices (or MP3 players as they're better known) out there for you to download music to, as well as films, games and pictures. Without a device, it's like having a roll of film without a camera to put it in. The only thing is, choosing which camera can be a little tricky.

To get digital music on to a portable device, you require two things: a computer (PC or Mac) and a software application that lets you play, store, organise, copy, convert and transfer digital files, whether they are old-fashioned word documents, photos, videos or, of course, songs. The software allows you to turn your computer and your digital audio device into your very own personal jukebox.

The four most popular software applications, which work with a whole host of digital audio players, are currently Apple's iTunes, Windows Media Player, WinAmp and RealPlayer.

A lot of devices will also come pre-packed with their own software applications. If you buy a Sony MP3 player, for example, you will also be supplied with their own software called Sonic Stage. Devices such as mobile phones will often come with their own software too.

These packages – iTunes, Windows Media Player, WinAmp and RealPlayer – all provide the same kind of functions: you can rip CDs, digitise the music, store it on your computer and organise it into a library; purchase music from the web; share music; and create playlists and copy them to a blank CD (say, to play in the car) and to your music player. You can also store video files, access radio stations from across the world, and learn about new music through what are known as recommendation engines.

The most important difference between the varying types of software is that they save your music files as completely different types, and these file types will only work with certain players.

If you save music on to your hard drive using iTunes – that is, copying music from a CD into the Apple software – they are saved as either MP3 or AAC files, depending on what you have originally specified. If you use Windows Media Player you have the option of either WAV, WMA or MP3. Similarly, with RealPlayer, your files can be saved as RMA or MP3.

Each device will accept an MP3, provided it has been transferred using the company-specified software. However, most devices are designed to work more easily with the specified file type – you won't have any trouble trying to find ways to convert files yourself. The iPod works seamlessly with the iTunes software, which will save your music as AAC files.

If you purchase music from iTunes, it will automatically be wrapped in a technology called DRM (Digital Rights Management), which prevents you from moving your music on to a different type of device, for example, Creative's Zen Player.

Unfortunately you need to make a decision when purchasing a digital device: do you want an iPod, which will only work with iTunes and stops you moving your collection to a different player, or do you want to opt for a PC where most other devices will let you use Windows Media Player or RealPlayer? Your choice depends on which device suits you best.

Digital Audio Players

A digital audio player – more commonly referred to as an MP3 player – is a music player that carries a mini hard drive with a memory. The number of different songs it can hold depends on its memory size.

Consider that an average song is about four minutes long. On a CD, that song would equate to using forty megabytes of space on your hard drive – if it hasn't been compressed using music software. When the song is saved as an MP3, WMA or AAC file, it is reduced in size: that is, compressed. An MP3 file reduces a song to around four megabytes.

An hour of music is equal to roughly 64 megabytes (MB) of storage space. A music listener who has an MP3 player with 1 gigabyte (GB, approximately 1,000 MB) capacity can store roughly 15 hours of music – a total of around 250 songs.

Popular Digital Audio Players On The Market

Digital audio players first arrived on the market in the late 1990s, when a company called Rio made available a player that carried about forty songs. Since then, various companies have launched digital music players: Sony, Creative, Samsung, Rio, Philips, iAudio and, of course, Apple with the iPod.

If you are a music obsessive, then chances are you are going to go for one of the biggest players – which can be anything up to 60GB (15,000 songs) – but for most people, a thousand songs is enough to be going on with and there are plenty of 4GB players out there, as well as ones which hold even less.

The iPod

Apple currently has five MP3 players on the market: two video iPods and three of its Nano brand, which have replaced their mini iPod. The success of the iPod can be measured by the fact that forty million iPods have been sold worldwide since their launch in 2000.

The two video iPods, to cope with the fact that video downloads are much larger in size, come with 30GB and 60GB memories. Like its smaller counterpart, the Nano, it's available in two colours, black and white.

The Nano range comes with three different memory sizes: 1GB, 2GB and 4GB. As you would expect, the larger the memory the higher the cost, with the larger video iPod being the most expensive. Sites such as eBay and Amazon sell iPods second-hand at a cheaper price, but to guarantee the best out of your iPod, it is best to buy one new.

All of the digital players in the iPod range have similar functions: you use a finger-sensitive wheel on the front to navigate between the different menus, while songs are organised into lists by artist, song name or even genre. You can also select songs by a 'most played' function, which records how many times you listen to each song.

Like all digital music players, the iPod allows you to create playlists of your favourite songs, so you can build a list, for example, of your twenty favourite rock songs, which will be stored in order for you. It's simply a case of putting it together in iTunes and then copying it over (more on this later).

A whole industry has built up around the iPod, with lots of companies offering iPod accessories. If you want to clip it to your arm in the gym, there are special attachments made especially for the purpose. If you are travelling and want to plug it into speakers, there are special devices on the market that pack into the smallest of spaces. If you want to use your iPod in the car, there is a cassette attachment to plug into your car stereo.

The Nano is a particularly small device – roughly the size of a credit card and as thin as an average pencil. The video iPod is slightly bigger to account for the 1.5-inch colour display.

Each iPod comes with earbud headphones, a USB 2.0 cable that connects it with your computer, a dock adapter to power it up from the mains, a QuickStart guide and a CD with iTunes for Mac and PC.

Other digital audio players

Aside from Apple's iPod, three other companies have proved to be very popular on the digital device market and all three work seamlessly with Windows Media Player – but not with Apple's iTunes.

Creative, Rio and Sony have all introduced a wide range of digital audio players and, unlike the iPod, you get a huge choice of options: memory sizes range from less than 1GB through to 10GB, while a lot of them supply the devices in a variety of colours.

Creative Zen Players

Creative has by far the largest choice of music players and consumer reviews on the web hail their products as easy to use, giving value for money and high quality. Under the brand name Zen it has a range of five different players: the Original, Touch, Micro, Neon and Sleek, all of which are competitively priced.

Choosing which Creative player you go for depends on various features. If you are seeking ultimate sound quality then the Zen Original prides itself on almost CD-like sound. If you are looking for a large memory and ease of use, then the Touch and Sleek are perfect – they come with 20GB and 40GB memories. However, if you are looking for something smaller and cheaper with, for example, a built-in radio, then the Micro, which comes with 4GB, 5GB and 6GB memory capacity, is ideal. It has won numerous awards for design and ease of use, namely from respected technology website CNet, which gave the Micro its Editors Choice Award.

The jewel in the Creative crown – and the major competitor to the iPod Photo – is the Zen Vision, which is a bit more pricey. Its hard disk holds up to 15,000 songs, thousands of photos or up to 120 hours of digital video. The Zen Vision plays WMV (Windows Media film files) and MPEG (the equivalent to MP3 for film) movies.

All Creative players will work with your computer in a number of ways: they are compatible with Windows Media Player and accept WMA and MP3 files, but will also work with online download services like Napster (see digital service providers). In fact, Napster struck an agreement with Creative that means that you can easily transfer songs you have purchased over from their system.

Creative also supplies its own software, Creative Media Source. One of the benefits of using Media Source is that it will transfer MP3 files over to your player with ease: something that can be a little tricky using Windows Media Player, which insists that everything is converted into a WMA file. So, if you have downloaded an MP3 from the web or are uploading a collection from your CD library, load and save it into Creative Media Source and with one drag of the file, it will load onto your player.

Sony
In the last couple of years Sony has extended its Walkman range to include two hard-disk digital audio players: the NW-A3000 and the NW-A1000. The devices come in two sizes, 20GB and 6GB. They are among the sleekest on the market and, unlike others, which have adopted a flat, boxlike design, the Sony is a rounded little machine which feels like a pod in your pocket. Both models come in three colours: grey, black and purple.

However, while they are sexy-looking gadgets, reports suggest that the Sony players are not that easy to use. While they all boast exceptional features like 35 hours of battery life (the average time for an iPod or Creative is 16 hours before you will need to recharge) and a 'Time Machine' shuffle, which will play your songs randomly from a pre-selected year, the problem is the software you are forced to use, Sony SonicStage. This works in conjunction with Sony's equivalent of the iTunes music store, Sony Connect.

Both of the players will only accept MP3s and Sony's proprietary file type, ATRAC (which is similar to Apple's AAC format). In order to transfer your music collection – whether it has been ripped from CD or purchased on the web – to a Sony player, you will have to use Connect. You can't simply lift songs out of Windows Media Player or RealPlayer, as you can with Creative, or many other devices. SonicStage is not the simplest piece of software to use, and reports have noted that it has a tendency to crash your PC.

Often it makes sense to go online and check out feedback from other people who have already purchased the player you are looking to buy. Good review websites include CNet, ZDNet and epinions.com.

iRiver
The iRiver series of digital audio players includes three players: the 20GB in red, the 6GB in grey and the 4GB in black.

What differentiates the players from others is the fact that they all automatically store photos as well as music and, as a bonus, all have an integrated radio. Other devices, such as the iPod and some of the Creative range, often insist you buy a separate radio attachment if you want to pick up FM radio.

The iRiver H10 series is also very flexible in terms of the file types it accepts. It will take MP3s and WMA files, meaning that you can use software such as Windows Media Player and RealPlayer. The iRiver also comes with its own software – Media Manager – which converts and compresses all music into a file type called ASF, which was developed by Microsoft. The chances of the iRiver failing to work with your PC, therefore, are very, very slim. It should be a seamless job!

Rio

The first company to launch a digital music player, Rio are among the most competitively priced on the market. The player with the largest memory is the Rio Carbon 6GB – not the largest, by far, but it still holds a substantial 1,500 songs.

The others – the Carbon Pearl (also 6GB), the 5GB and the ce2100 (2.5GB) all come with the Windows Media 'Plays For Sure' guarantee, meaning that they function seamlessly with Windows Media Player. The ce2100 has one of the smallest memories on the market for a hard-disk player, holding just over 300 songs.

The players also boast that they are no bigger than the iPod Nano – not much bigger than a business card – and have a 20-hour battery life, which must have contributed to them winning PC World's World Class award.

The companies listed above may be the ones we have become most familiar with, but there are a whole host of other technology manufacturers producing digital audio players running on a hard-disk memory. One, iAudio, produces what is currently the smallest hard-disk player on the market, which carries 1,000 songs, while a lesser known company called Vusys has manufactured the I-DJ670, which allows you to record MP3 directly from CDs played on your stereo – it's simply a case of plugging in a line-in cable from the player to your hi-fi – no need for transfer via software! It might also be worth looking at companies such as Philips, MobiBLU and Archos, which provide a range of players at very competitive prices.

Flash players

If the iPod Shuffle has caught your eye then you've been tempted by what is known as a flash player – a digital audio device which doesn't have a hard disk, but instead has a smaller flash drive. One of the benefits of a flash drive is that you can virtually stamp on it or throw it out of a window and it won't break. It also means that songs won't skip if you're on the treadmill, for example. However, the catch is that they have much smaller memory capacities.

The small flash device is naturally lightweight and rewritable, meaning that you can delete files on it as many times as you like. The most popular retail sizes are somewhere between 512MB (half 1GB) and 4GB.

A flash drive is also known as a USB key, which means it will plug directly into the USB drive in your computer: beware though, PCs that run on Windows 95 or 98 rarely recognise flash devices – you will have to download a 'plug-in' in order for your computer to recognise that something has been plugged into it.

Flash drives are also known as pen drives, chip sticks, thumb drives, USB keys and memory sticks.

There are vast arrays of flash-based digital audio players on the market, which can also act as portable storage devices for documents, photos, address books, etc. Because they are smaller than a hard-disk device, they are a lot less expensive.

Apple iPod Shuffle

The iPod Shuffle is a very nifty little device. Weighing about as much as a door key, it contains a memory of up to 1GB (a 512MB version is also available) and charges in four hours. If playlists are your thing, then the Shuffle is ideal – with one flick of a switch (found on the edge of the player), it will randomly play all of the songs you have transferred over.

The Shuffle works seamlessly with iTunes, on which you will find an option called Autofill. When you select this option, iTunes, rather cleverly, will fill your Shuffle to the brim with a random selection of songs from your library. If you prefer to listen to whole albums, simply flick the switch the other way and the Shuffle will play all of your songs in your chosen order.

As a flash device – so it doesn't skip – it is ideal for using in the gym, while jogging and even dancing! It is also so small it will slide into the pocket of your jeans. With a low price point, it is a great starter option for anyone who wishes to get into downloading.

Other Flash Devices

Creative have an extensive flash-player range including the MuVo line and the cheekily named Zen Nano Plus.

The Creative MuVo Micro N200 is the sleekest in the range. Incredibly thin in design, it accepts MP3 and WMA files, but its best selling point is that it can be plugged into the back of a stereo and will record CDs directly. It also comes with an FM tuner, voice/FM recording and hours of battery life. For the more style conscious, it comes in eight different colours and a range of memory capacities: 128MB, 256MB, 512MB and 1GB. There is one problem, however. If you have devised a playlist and wish to transfer it, the player will automatically list your songs in alphabetical order. So if you are a little fussy about your playlists, then this might not be the ideal device for you.

If you compare the Creative Zen Nano Plus with the iPod Shuffle, the first thing you will notice is that it comes with an LED-display, which lets you see which track is playing, who it's by and which genre of music it falls into: something the Shuffle doesn't have.

Like the Shuffle though, it is a pretty sexy device. The sound quality is renowned for being particularly good, while the small 'wheel' on the side of the player allows you to scroll through tracks with ease – one push of the wheel and the track will play.

The device will accept playlists, but like hard-disk players, it will not allow you to select playlists on the go – that is, you have to put them together on your computer before transferring them. Hard-disk devices will normally allow you to create a playlist directly on the device itself.

The Creative Zen Nano Plus accepts MP3 and WMA files, as well as containing 32 preset radio stations, and comes in a choice of ten colours.

Sony has really stepped up its game in the field of flash players. Its NW-E400 collection is not only a very fashionable-looking range, but each device contains 50 hours of battery life, compared to 12 hours on the iPod Shuffle. The NW-E400 and E500 ranges vary in price, but will carry both MP3s and the company's proprietary format, ATRAC. They also charge in a very speedy three hours. If you are looking for a trendy device, which will carry 250 songs at most, this could be a brilliant option.

Other brands out there include Samsung, SanDisk (who are relatively new to the market, but have already established themselves with flash memory cards), iRiver, Philips and Panasonic, to name just a few. It is worth checking out websites such as Engadget, CNet and even Amazon to read customer reviews and find something to suit your needs and your budget. All of the companies above come with high recommendations.

PERSONAL
MEDIA
PLAYERS

While you might only be interested in carrying music on the go, there are many devices on the market that do a whole lot more. So, if you're keen on downloading films, your photos, games and so forth, as well as your music collection, it might be wise to invest in a portable media player that will allow you to do all of the above.

The benefits of portable media players are that they come with colour screens, much bigger memories than digital audio players, as well as the ability to play games and view photos. The high-quality LCD screen on a portable media player means that, for now at least, they aren't particularly small devices – quite often they will be the size of a paperback book and weigh almost as much as two iPods.

Interestingly, Apple does not necessarily have the lead in this field and recent launches from Sony – with the PSP – and the Creative Zen Vision are proving to be equally as popular as the Apple iPod Media Player, which was made famous by the company's sponsorship deal with U2.

Apple iPod Media Player

The iPod media player (the fifth-generation iPod device) comes in two sizes, the 30GB and 60GB models, which can hold up to 15,000 songs, full-colour album art and up to 25,000 photos, or 150 hours of video viewable on a 2.5-inch colour display.

Where Apple had been criticised before for lack of battery life, the iPod media player boasts up to twenty hours of battery life – five hours more than any of its predecessors in the Apple range.

Plus, with the new media iPod, you get a bigger display and one more iPod colour – black. At less than half an inch thick, the 30GB iPod takes up about 45 per cent less room than the original iPod. Even the 60GB model is thinner than the fourth-generation 30GB iPod.

Creative Zen Vision M

The Zen Vision only comes in one size, 30GB, and so has less storage capacity than the mammoth 60GB iPod. On average, it can hold up to 120 hours of video in a wide variety of formats, which is where it has a slight edge over the Apple device. Video file types compatible with the Zen Vision include DivX, MPEG1, MPEG2, MPEG4 and WMV saved on version 9 and upwards on Windows Media Player.

If you were to use half of its memory for video (60 hours), it would be possible to store a further 7,500 songs. Obviously this would reduce if you also chose to store your photo collection on it.

The device is relatively light, comes with a 2.5-inch colour display, has up to fourteen hours of battery life and, if you're style conscious, is available in five colours: blue, green, pink, black and white.

The Zen Vision also comes with some nifty bonuses: it can be connected to a projector or TV with a video cable for viewing on a big screen, and it also has an integrated FM radio with 32 preset stations.

Prices on the web show that the Creative Vision M is similar in price to the iPod.

Sony PSP

The portable Playstation is the device to buy if you want to play games on the go, since reviews suggest that, as a portable gaming device, it is well ahead of its competitors on many levels. If gaming isn't your thing, the PSP can also be used as a straightforward media player.

The PSP is a pretty heavy device, mainly because it is dominated by an impressive 4.3-inch colour display. The screen has a 16:9 wide-screen aspect ratio, so it is ideal for watching videos and film.

More like a mini-computer, the PSP has external drives that can be used to load up films and music. Films for PSP can be purchased on a format called Universal Media Disc and slotted into a drive on the side of the player. You can also plug in a USB Memory Stick and load up files from there, whether they are music, video, films, TV shows or photos.

There are a variety of ways in which you can load up files on to the PSP. It automatically comes with Sony's proprietary software, SonicStage, but a whole raft of companies have also created software that works with the PSP – Sony's software is not the only toolset for getting music or movies onto a PSP. A quick scout around the web will find alternatives including Media Boss, PSP Movie Creator, PSP Video Express, Xcopy9, PSPWare, iPSP, Mobile Media Maker, PSP Video 9, 3GP Converter and PSP Multimedia Extender – all of which allow you to convert and transfer files to and from the PSP's memory stick, which is then slotted into the player.

The player will accept a variety of file types and was recently upgraded to take AAC audio files, ATRAC3+ audio files from a Memory Stick, MPEG video files (if encoded using a proprietary Sony encoding), as well as view gif, bitmap, tiffs and MP3 file types.

Being more than a simple audio player, the PSP can also connect to the internet, via a wireless connection. All in all, even though there has been the odd complaint about battery life, the PSP is a pretty marvellous multifaceted machine. The price depends upon the extras you might buy with it.

Sony HMPA-1

Not quite on sale in Europe yet, but already a hit in the US and Japan, it's a smaller device than the Creative and iPod with a 20GB memory. However, on the plus side, it has been very well designed. Extremely sleek and stylish, it comes with a 3.5-inch display, an inch bigger than its counterparts.

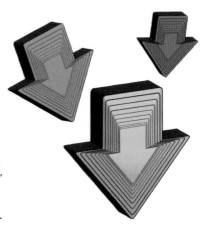

What's more, the Sony HMPA-1 will accept virtually any file type, including WMA, MP3, MPEG, JPEG, WMV and AAC (Apple!) among others, unlike the company's digital audio players, which will only take Sony's proprietary ATRAC codec.

There is a small catch, however. When files are transferred on to the HMPA-1 they are converted into an undisclosed proprietary format, which means that if you switch them back into, for example, iTunes or Windows Media Player, the software refuses to recognise the file and play it back.

Video files are automatically converted into MPEGs, but can take some time to load – a thirty-minute TV show can take up to nearly half a gigabyte's worth of memory and will slow down your PC quite dramatically. (Small tip – if you are transferring over a large file then close down all other applications on your computer, otherwise it might crash.)

Personal media players accept a variety of file types (also known as 'codecs') for both video and pictures. Here's a brief summary.

Digital Video File Types
MPEG: Like MP3, MPEG is a standard and generic file type developed by the Moving Picture Experts Group. This video file is designed to be the digital equivalent of VHS quality and will normally work with all portable media players.

WMV: This is the Microsoft video file type (like the Windows counterpart for audio, WMA), meaning that if your portable media player runs on Windows software, this will be the file type it accepts and works most efficiently with.

ASF: This file type is also Windows-based and it is essentially the 'wrapping' around a WMV file. This means the file will contain extra information – metadata (song title, artist, genre, etc.) – and can also store Digital Rights Management, which will control how you can use that file (see below for more on DRM).

DivX: This is a video codec created by a company called DivX Inc., which means it is an independent file type that can work across a variety of devices and does not keep you bound to either Windows or Apple. It has become popular because long videos can be compressed digitally into small sizes without losing quality.

Image File Types

Jpeg: This is a file type that refers to an image. It is the most widely used image file type on the web since it compresses images into small sizes, making them easier to transfer and store. If compressed properly, a jpeg will maintain a good standard of quality for viewing on the web or a portable media player. Impressively, it has the capacity to store up to sixteen million hues of colour.

Bitmaps: Another image file type that interprets colours, when compressed, into three groups: red, green and blue. Bitmap images can often be pixelated (making them less clear), but they are ideal for low-resolution graphics or logos.

Gifs: A gif is a bitmap image format that can contain up to 256 distinct colours. Like jpegs and bitmaps, gifs are compressed files, and were adopted to reduce the amount of time it takes to transfer images over a network connection.

What is DRM?

DRM stands for Digital Rights Management. It is a piece of technology which, when embedded into a codec or file type, controls the way in which you can use that file. Companies will use DRM for many different reasons. For example, if you purchase a music track from Apple's iTunes store, it will be wrapped in the company's FairPlay DRM. The FairPlay DRM will prevent you from transferring that song, or playing it on any other device other than an iPod. It also limits the amount of times you can burn that file to a CD and whether or not you can share it with your friends via email.

Quite often, DRM is placed upon a film file or a music file by the record or film companies. Even some CDs will these days come with some form of DRM, meaning that you cannot rip the CD to your computer.

There is a lot of debate about whether DRM is a good thing, since it prevents you from having the freedom to use a digital file how you want. It is a sensible idea to check if your digital audio player or personal media player accepts DRM files.

MOBILE
PHONES

Within the last couple of years, the popularity of ringtones, and the success of the iPod, has led handset makers and the mobile phone operators to start incorporating music players into mobile phones.

Many music-enabled phones have now been launched on to the market, allowing you to download songs, over the air, to your phone. Songs can also be 'side-loaded' on to mobiles, from your PC, via a cable that's a bit like a USB. Mobile phone music downloads do have their limitations for now, but will definitely improve as time goes on.

In a lot of instances, the cost of an over-the-air download is pretty expensive since you will pay for both the audio file and its transmission over the network – what's known as a data charge.

Even if your phone comes with the facility to side-load audio files, there are not that many phones with the memory to cope with much more than 100 songs.

Each mobile device will work differently according to its manufacturer and each mobile network will offer a different type of music service. Depending on which type of handset you have, what you will be able to access will differ.

Popular Mobile Devices That Support Music

Both Nokia and Sony Ericsson have invested greatly in manufacturing mobile phones that support music files. The Sony Ericsson Walkman phone has been pitched at the market as more of a music player than an actual phone, while the Nokia N91 boasts that it can hold up to 3,000 songs – way above anything any of the other handsets can deliver!

Here's a rundown of some of the most popular mobile music devices on the market.

Nokia N91

The Nokia N91 music phone is targeted at those who want their music and images available on the move – its main feature is its 4GB memory. The MP3 player on the N91 supports a number of file types: MP3, AAC, AAC+, WAV and WMA.

The four-way navigation pad on the keypad sleeve directly controls the MP3 playback and enables you to browse your library of music. You can also add your own favourite headphones or speakers, as a 3.5mm jack has been provided. It also comes with an inbuilt FM radio supporting Visual Radio, the system that gives you images and information relating to the track playing on air.

As with all devices, tracks can be side-loaded on to the device with the software the phone comes with. However, you can also download tracks over the air from your network provider (more on that later).

Nokia N70

This is a popular music device, although if you compare its 30MB of memory with the N91's 4GB, it's easy to see how limiting this device can be. Nokia teamed up with music software experts RealPlayer to provide the back-end technology on this phone that lets you listen to music and watch video clips, so it's a very straightforward experience. It also supports, like the N91, a wide variety of file types: MP3, AAC, Real Audio, WAV, Nokia Ring Tones, gifs and bitmaps.

Nokia 6680
This one carries even less memory – only 10MB – and, like the N70, also runs on RealPlayer software. It supports and plays many multimedia files (video and music) including RealMedia (Real Video and Real Audio), MP3 and AAC.

Sony Ericsson W900i
The W900i was the first 3G (more about 3G later) music mobile phone with enough memory, software and features to rival any mobile phone or MP3 player on the market.

Its memory is almost half a gigabyte – a total of 125 songs, which equates to the same as most flash players on the market – and this can be expanded by inserting a 2GB memory card. Mobile flash cards are sold in most phone or electrical shops.

Branded 'Walkman', it's designed to be as much of a mobile music device as it is a mobile phone and comes with ready-to-run music transfer software. With it, you can copy music from an audio CD or digital music on your PC to your phone. It's a very quick and easy process – much like transferring songs on to, say, an iPod.

Sony Ericsson W700i/W800i

These phones are similar to the W900i, but aren't 3G, meaning that over-the-air downloads are going to take so much time as to make it virtually impossible.

Still, the W700i has plenty of storage room for your favourite music, which has to be stored on a 256MB (up to 64 songs) memory card you'll find included in the box. And when you need to store more, you can do so by purchasing a 4GB Memory Stick™ PRO Duo (again, available from outlets selling the phone). The W800i comes with a slightly larger memory card – a 512MB Memory Stick™ PRO Duo, which can be upgraded for a 1GB version. The entire range accepts MP3 and MPEG4 files for audio and video.

Motorola RAZR vx3 and RAZR v3

Motorola's top of the range 3G music phone is the RAZR v3x. It accepts MP3, AAC and MPEG4 player – with stereo surround sound, no less – and has 64MB of internal memory, expandable up to 512 MB with a memory card.

The RAZR v3 supports all kinds of ringtones and video, but isn't designed to play full-track audio downloads.

Samsung D800

Samsung have not, as yet, brought out a 3G phone specifically designed for music like Nokia, Sony Ericsson and Motorola. However, the D800 does have a music player that accepts MP3, AAC, AAC+, e-AAC+ and WMA, and also comes pre-installed with 64 polyphonic ringtones (more about ringtones later). It has an 80MB internal music memory, which cannot be expanded with memory cards. The D820 comes with 73MB of internal memory, but will also accept memory cards.

Siemens SL75

The integrated media player offers MP3, AAC+ and video playing in excellent quality. The 58MB internal memory isn't huge, but enough to carry forty songs or so. It's good if you just want to carry a couple of albums around with you.

What is 3G?

The simplest way to understand 3G is to imagine that you have a wireless, broadband pipe flowing straight into your mobile phone. The old network, 2.5G, which most of us still use, was perfectly adequate for making calls and maybe checking out information on WAP portals and downloading ringtones but, as many of you probably noticed, it wasn't that quick and would often cut out. It proved to be more irritating than useful.

3G – which will be offered by your network provider – can only work if you have a 3G-enabled device. Many of the mobile devices listed above work more effectively on the 3G network. Mobile operator 3, which is UK-based only, is an example of a network that has embraced 3G and has grown increasingly popular because users have been able to download audio and video directly to their phones while on the move, very quickly!

3G enables you to transmit voice, data – including video and audio files – and images. To get slightly technical, 3G improves data transmission speed up to 144Kbps (kilobytes per second) in a high-speed moving environment, 384Kbps in a low-speed moving environment, and 2Mbps (megabytes per second) in a stationary environment. By 'environment' we mean where you are at the time. 3G is currently being rolled out across the UK, but different areas will have different speeds. If you are in the city, then it's likely to be ultra fast, but if you're out in the Hebrides, it may well be a little slower. Like the internet, a heavy load of people using 3G means that it can sometimes slow down, but this is often unnoticeable.

If you have a 3G phone you will be able to stream audio and video, as well as download as if you were on the web.

While 3G was 'the future' a couple of years ago, the mobile networks are already working on faster connections and soon will be introducing HSDPA – a boost to the 3G network that will increase the speed of 3G by up to eight times!

What is Bluetooth?

No doubt you have purchased a mobile phone in the past and in the guide it has mentioned Bluetooth capability. Bluetooth – named after the tenth-century Danish King Bluetooth, who encouraged warring factions to negotiate peace – is an industry-standard piece of technology installed into mobile phones, PDAs and computers that allows you to share information.

By activating the Bluetooth function on your mobile you can 'pair' with another mobile within a 100m range and swap files such as MP3s and video files, as well as ringtones and pictures. It is a free application, so if you're with friends and want to share something, it's simply a case of activating the Bluetooth function!

Most mobile phones will give you the option, when you select a certain file (music, video, or picture) either to send via MMS, email, text message, or share via Bluetooth. Note, however, that if you have side-loaded a song on to your phone, it is actually illegal to share it with another person as this is considered to be copyright infringement.

It is also probable that if you have downloaded files, such as music, over the air from your network provider, they will be bound with some form of DRM. In the telecoms industry, most music files are wrapped in something called OMA (Open Mobile Alliance) DRM, which will prevent you from sharing your songs with your friends via text, email or Bluetooth. The OMA DRM will also stop you from moving the song you have purchased to any other type of music device, such as an iPod.

Flash/Memory Cards

As we've mentioned before, it is possible to buy memory cards to expand the memory on your mobile phone. Some phones will have a 'docking port' somewhere on the side, which, when opened, acts as a slot for memory cards.

Memories, or flash cards as they are sometimes known, have also been adopted by record labels to offer you music that can be exported from the card into your mobile phone. For example, a memory card manufacturer called SanDisk teamed up with Virgin Records to produce a Rolling Stones memory card, which can be slotted into your mobile. The card comes with a selection of the band's greatest hits, pictures and video clips all ready for you to download to your mobile.

Similarly, T-Mobile struck a deal with EMI and Robbie Williams' management firm to produce a special memory card for his last album, making available a selection of songs, ringtones, icons and pictures specifically designed for mobile usage.

Ringtones

Ringtones have been one of the biggest fads in mobile downloading. More money is spent on them than actual CD singles these days. It is practically impossible to list all of the many retail outlets selling ringtones and their various incarnations such as polyphonic tones (where the ringtone is a closer replica to the original song), truetones/realtones (which is the actual piece of music cut down especially to make a ringtone) and ringback tones (they replace the dialling tone when you are put through to someone's mobile, so instead of hearing a 'beep', you hear that person's current favourite piece of music).

It is even possible to make your own ringtones. Some CD singles come with the option for you to edit a song and then transfer that clip to your mobile.

All of the mobile networks offer a ringtone selection, either via a WAP site accessible on your mobile, or direct from the networks' website. There is also the option of buying from other registered ringtone providers such as Jamster (who were made famous by the Crazy Frog ringtone), MobTV, Vizzavi and mobiletones.com.

It is advised that you check first of all whether a ringtone is compatible with your mobile phone. Some mobiles won't accept certain ringtones, depending on where they have been purchased from.

Transferring Digital Files to a Personal Media Player

Unless you are using an iPod – the photo iPod could be considered a portable media player, for example – chances are your device will be compatible with Windows Media Player 10, as most digital audio devices are. This is a straightforward guide to how you can transfer your files from your PC to your chosen device. Most work in very similar ways. If you are using an iPod, you will have to use Apple's iTunes.

Using Windows Media Player

Make sure you have Windows Media Player 10 installed on your PC.

- Use the USB cable (these will come with your portable player) to connect your device to your computer.

- Windows Media Player automatically detects that your portable device is plugged in and asks you to sync the player with the Windows Media Player software.

- At this stage, it prompts you to run a set-up so that both the player and the software can 'talk' to each other.

- The Sync Wizard will automatically launch – run through the options (it's best to select all of the default options, unless you are more familiar with the advanced options). Click finish.

- If you have been saving all of your music (whether ripped from CD, or gathered from the internet), it will appear in the Media Library option in the menu on the left. Check in here to make sure the files you want to copy are in the system.

- Select 'Copy to CD or Device' option in the left-hand menu.

- A window with a split-screen will appear. In the top left is a button called 'Items to Copy', and underneath is what appears to be a yellow head. Click on this to select the files you want to copy. Once selected, they will appear in the left side of the split screen.

- Each file will come up with a tick-box next to it. If there is a file in there you don't want to copy, de-select the tick.

- Above the right-hand side split-screen is a button saying 'Items On Device' — click on this to select your digital audio, or personal media player. It should be listed among other 'drives' on your computer.

- Once it is selected, hit the red copy button on the top right of the screen.

- That's you finished!

Note: File conversion may be necessary for some audio and video files to make them compatible with your player. However, when you upload a file into either iTunes or Windows Media Player, for example an MP3 or MPEG, the software should automatically convert it into a compatible file, such as WMV, WMA or AAC.

If you find that iTunes or Windows will not convert your file, then sometimes it's best to use the transfer software that comes with your player. This will convert the file, and you can either use it to transfer the file to your player, or save that file and copy it into your iTunes or Windows library.

How to Create a Playlist in Windows Media Player

- **Open Windows Media Player.**

- **Select the 'Media Library' option in the main menu on the left-hand side.**

- **At the top of the window in the left-hand corner is a button called 'Playlists' – click on it.**

- **Select 'New Playlist'.**

- **A split-screen will launch in a new window. On the left is an option to 'View Media Library'; select this and choose from one of three options – by artist, album or genre.**

- **It doesn't matter which one you pick (by clicking on the 'yellow head'), you can use this to bring up the individual songs.**

● Select your track by clicking on it twice and it will flick over into the right-hand side of the split-screen.

● Continue doing this until you have built up enough songs on your list. Note that if you are burning a playlist to a CD, you can only fit around twenty songs on one CD. If you are copying to a digital audio player, then your choice can be much wider.

● To change the order of the songs on your playlist, select a song by highlighting it with the mouse and use the up and down arrows at the bottom of the right-hand split-screen to move it accordingly.

● To delete a song from your playlist, highlight in the right-hand screen, right-click your mouse and select 'Delete from Playlist' – be careful not to select the other option, 'Delete from Media Library', because you will lose it altogether from the Windows Media application.

Creating a Playlist in iTunes

● Open iTunes.

● Select 'File' from the main menu at the top of the screen.

● Select 'New Playlist'.

● In the navigation bar on the left, a new 'untitled playlist' icon appears. If you have existing or pre-set playlists, the new one will be alphabetically ordered under 'u' for 'untitled'.

● It might make sense to name the playlist, to avoid confusion with others. Do this by clicking on the icon and tapping it in the highlighted box.

- To build the playlist, you need to be in the 'Library' — where all your audio files are stored.

- When in the Library, it's a simple case of dragging your files over with the mouse and dropping them on to the playlist icon.

- There's a more fiddly alternative if you are running iTunes on the PC — when you highlight the track, you can also right-click and use the sub-menu option 'Add To Playlist'.

- If you want to copy a consecutive run of tracks from one album to a playlist, highlight the first selection, then the last while holding down the shift key. You can then drag and drop that whole block into a playlist.

- To change the order of the songs in your playlist, highlight the track you want to move, hold down the mouse and drag up or down to a new position in the running order.

- To delete a track from your list, highlight the track and press the delete key. The track will be removed from the playlist only, NOT from your library.

- If you want to delete a whole playlist, highlight the list in the side vertical menu and then press the delete key on your keyboard.

- You can create a playlist from scratch from any track you have selected. In the Library window, highlight the track, select the 'File' option menu from the top menu bar, and then select 'New Playlist From Selection'. A new playlist, titled the same as that track title, will appear in the vertical side menu, in the playlist section. You can then add other tracks in the usual way, and rename it accordingly.

● To rename a playlist, select it from the vertical side menu, then double-click and type the new name straight in.

Transferring Playlists/Files to an iPod

● Connect your iPod to the computer via the USB cable.

● The iPod icon and its name will appear in the left-hand vertical side menu of iTunes. (This is called the Source menu, and it has the word 'Source' at its head.)

● To add an existing iTunes Library Playlist to your iPod, simply drag and drop the playlist name on to the iPod icon.

● As you drag, the playlist's name will be highlighted with a blue background and as you move it over, a green plus sign will appear.

● As it goes in successfully, it will immediately appear in the iPod Playlist.

DOWNLOADING TO YOUR HOME COMPUTER

Let's look at downloading individual songs or albums to your home computer, whether it be a PC or a Mac.

There is a whole host of ways to get hold of music on the internet. Since 2001, an array of legal download sites has launched – mainly to suppress the thriving illegal download business that had caused a right stink at the start of the millennium.

Illegal file sharing, also known as peer-to-peer or P2P, is still a mainstay of the internet and continues to be one of the biggest distribution channels for music.

What Exactly is File Sharing?

File sharing allows you to swap files, stored on your home computer, with other people hooked up to the internet. To make this happen, you will have downloaded a peer-to-peer client such as Limewire, Gnutella or BearShare. A peer-to-peer client is basically a piece of software – usually available as a free download from the web – which opens up your hard drive to other people looking for music, games and film files on the web.

A peer-to-peer client allows you to search for files – for example, you can tap in the name of your favourite artist or song and it will search other users on that network to see if they have it. The more popular the peer-to-peer client, the more chance your favourite song will be on it, as more users will be hooked up.

It will also allow you, in some cases, to play that song before it is saved to your hard drive, so if it is a corrupt file and doesn't work you needn't save it. Peer-to-peer clients will run your search and return with a number of options, such as the song performed by different people, or stored in different file sizes – you can choose the smaller files over the larger ones so as not to fill up the memory on your hard drive. Files on peer-to-peer networks are invariably MP3 and, of course, have no DRM. This means they can usually be transferred to any device - sometimes through software provided by the device manufacturer, sometimes not.

Sounds too good to be true? In a sense, it is. While it is the ultimate distribution network for music, throwing open access to the world's biggest library of songs, it is illegal. What's more, governments, record labels, film companies and more organisations besides are well and truly on to it. File sharing is copyright infringement. While you are not paying for the song or film, the record label or film company isn't receiving any money, and – naturally enough – they're not too happy about that.

Since the launch and subsequent closure of Napster – in its original incarnation as a peer-to-peer service, and before the name was snapped up by a web-savvy company keen to launch a legal alternative – in 1999, all of the world's biggest 'creative' firms have got out their big legal guns to shut down these operations, and fine those using them. Individuals have been fined for carrying a lot of files on their hard drives and making them available to other web users. Users of peer-to-peer networks can be tracked down through their IP address, which Internet Service Providers have been forced to disclose.

Meanwhile, although peer-to-peer file sharing might seem like the most exhilarating joyride a music fan could ever take, it comes with another pitfall. To fund these pieces of software, the owners build in advertising, and the networks can also sometimes become corrupt with adware and spyware. These applications can do more than crash your computer – they can wipe the whole of your hard drive.

Legal Alternatives to Peer-to-peer

While the closure of Napster (version one) was happening, various parties were putting together plans to launch legal alternatives. While none of them work on a peer-to-peer system (although legalised peer-to-peer is something we will see very soon), they all offer downloads of individual tracks and albums plus, in some instances, subscription services – which seem certain to form a substantial part of music distribution in the future. Most of them allow you to build playlists and download them either to a PC, a nominated digital audio player, or both.

Here is a selection of them.

Bignoisemusic

Bignoisemusic is an Oxfam-backed service powered by OD2 that launched in the UK in May 2004. With 10 per cent of sales going to charity, the site has supported the Sudan appeal. Music from all the major labels and many independents is delivered in the protected WMA format.

www.bignoisemusic.com

Bleep

Warp Records' Bleep.com sells DRM-free MP3 downloads from many of the UK's top independent labels such as Domino, One Little Indian, Beggars, Ninja Tune and Warp itself, allowing access to the catalogues of artists such as Franz Ferdinand, Bjork, Roots Manuva and Aphex Twin.
www.bleep.com

Sony Connect

Connect is Sony's own download service, and is integrated with Sony's own SonicStage music software that comes with its devices. All tracks are formatted in Sony's ATRAC3 format, which means they will not work on any other device except for a Sony and cannot be played in iTunes or Windows Media Player.
www.connect-europe.com

Download at Woolworths.co.uk

A basic, easy-to-navigate download site that is perfect if you want to download chart stuff only, but the chances of you finding that rare song you heard once in the 1970s is zilch. Files come as protected WMA files, which means they have a certain amount of DRM wrapped around them – this will limit how many computers you can transfer the file to and how many times it can be burned to CD.
www.woolworths.co.uk/download

eMusic US

This is a US-based subscriber download site that focuses solely on supplying music from independent labels. If your taste is a little bit more obscure, chances are you're going to find what you're looking for here.

It was the first website on the planet to sell MP3s and consequently has gained quite a reputation for itself. It now carries more than a million songs, which can be downloaded as MP3, WMA and iTunes-compatible AAC files. That's right – you can use eMusic to fill up your iPod.

You're not able to just log on and buy individual songs, but you can subscribe for only a small amount each month, which entitles you to forty free downloads and the chance to listen to any song in the eMusic library. You can also upgrade to more expensive packages, which allow you to do extra things like burn songs to CD or watch live performances from venues across the US.
www.emusic.com

HMV Digital

One of the big guns! HMV recently relaunched its download site and it is as slick as you can imagine, with a huge two-million-track catalogue, and not only can you pay for songs on a track-by-track basis, you can also buy a monthly subscription that entitles you to download as much music as you like. If you stop paying, however, they have special technology which will render your downloads dead! With much more besides, this is a flashy service. All files are WMA protected.
www.hmv.co.uk/digital

iTunes Music Store

The most famous digital music store in the world – this has had more marketing cash pushed into it than London's 2012 Olympics. This has one of the largest catalogues on the web, while its player ties in neatly with the world's most famous digital audio device – the iPod. All tracks are AAC files, which means they cannot be transferred to any device other than the iPod, although they can be transferred to other nominated computers and, within limits, burned to CD.
www.itunes.co.uk/com

Music Match

A purely US-based service, Music Match is backed by Microsoft and Yahoo and, consequently, all of the tracks are available to download as WMA or MP3 files.

The Music Match Jukebox 10 is a piece of software that works in exactly the same way as iTunes or Windows Media Player and therefore allows you to load up, organise, copy and create playlists from your music.

The software, which comes as a free download, is linked with the Music Match download shop, which carries one million songs.

There are some interesting features – you can stream up to 900,000 songs and access the pre-programmed radio shows, while the service is compatible with all digital audio players apart from the iPod.
www.musicmatch.com

Napster US/UK

Napster version 2.0 is a relaunched version of the illegal file-sharing network set up by uber-geek Shawn Fanning and was the first of the leading US sites to launch in the UK.

Napster's selling point is its subscription service. For a certain fee each month you can download and listen to as much music as you like from a catalogue of more than two million songs. If you pay just a little bit more each month, you can upgrade to Napster To Go, whereby all of the files you have downloaded can be transferred to a Napster-compatible player (most of the Creative range for starters). Once again, if you let your subscription expire, there is technology that cancels out all of your downloads and, once you synch your player with your PC, Napster will wipe out your player's Napster library. Extra fees apply when burning to disc or transferring to a digital player, while the downloads are encoded in the popular WMA format.

Napster also offers various pre-programmed radio stations, information on artists and up-and-coming bands, plus playlist recommendations. As a well-rounded music package, it doesn't really get much better.
www.napster.co.uk/com

Real Rhapsody US

Wow! Without wishing to single out one individual service above all of the others – this is it. Rhapsody is a beauty of a service and, unfortunately, currently only available to those in the US. This could change in 2007 but, for now, the rest of the world has to look on with envy.

Rhapsody is a subscription service, like eMusic and Napster, which offers a two-tiered pricing option. Pricewise it is very similar to other services. However, unlike eMusic (which only carries music from independent labels) and Napster, you can ask Rhapsody for almost any song and it will be there. Furthermore, if it's not there, it will still be listed and you'll be told why it's not in the library.

Other benefits of Rhapsody, which is compatible with any digital player apart from the iPod, include an easy-to-use playlist builder, a fantastic recommendation engine, the chance to listen to radio stations built around your favourite artists and, of course, the chance to listen to any track on the service whenever you want.
www.rhapsody.com

Tesco Download
Launched in November 2004, Tesco was the first UK supermarket to launch a download service in the UK. Much like Woolworths, it is an easy-to-use service specialising more in chart hits than anything else, so is not an ideal service if you are a music aficionado. All files are offered as WMA.
www.tescodownloads.com

TuneTribe
Tunetribe has only been around for a couple of years, but is already carving itself out a place in the market as a credible alternative to the big guns. It carries a library of major record-label content and independent music, plus a raft of unsigned music. Tracks vary in price and are offered up as both WMA and MP3 files.
www.tunetribe.com

Virgin Digital

Like HMV, Virgin relaunched its service in September 2005. It has similar features to the HMV online store (probably because both stores were, in the background, put together by the same people) – a huge catalogue of tracks, the option to buy tracks 'à la carte', a subscription offering, files offered as WMA, playlist recommendations, artist-specific features and offers, plus what is known as 'variable pricing', where you are likely to pay less for an older artist than something which is brand new. Like HMV, it is a very slick service that comes with its own player so, even before you have saved the track to your hard drive, you can listen to it through the site. Like Napster and HMV, it offers an all-you-can-eat subscription service, as well as a portable service. Songs can also be burned to CD.

www.virgindigital.com

Wippit

Wippit is one of the most endearing stories in the digital world. It is, by far, the oldest download site operating out of the UK and was originally the world's first licensed P2P network, until the record labels got all uppity about it.

Wippit now offers individual downloads on an 'à la carte' basis, some as cheap as 39p each, and is constantly offering all manner of deals. Unlike most download sites, files are encoded in both WMA and MP3, which gives you as much flexibility as you need. It's a site definitely worth checking out, since it also carries a pretty substantial library.

www.wippit.com

Other download services available to UK, US and Europe-based music fans

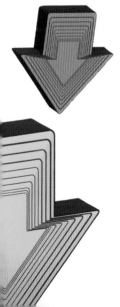

Classical Music Library: www.classical.com
easyMusic: www.easymusic.com
Freeserve Music Club: www.freeserve.com/musicclub
MetalTracks: www.metaltracks.com
Ministry of Sound: www.ministryofsound.com
MTV Digital Downloads: www.mtv.co.uk
Packard Bell Music Station: www.packardbell.co.uk/services/music/
Panasonic Music Stream: www.panasonicmusicstream.com
Playlouder: www.playlouder.com
Sonic Selector: www.sonicselector.com
Streets Online: www.streetsonline.co.uk/digital
Track it Down: www.trackitdown.net
Trax2burn: www.trax2burn.com
Uptown Records: www.uptownrecords.com
Vitaminic Music Club: www.vitaminic.co.uk
War Child: www.warchildmusic.com

Internet Service Providers (ISPs)

If you have the internet at home – as most of us do now – then you will be signed up to an ISP. The ISP will supply your internet connection as well as a portal – a place where your membership will get you access to a whole host of information and entertainment features. There are hundreds of ISPs – some offering a basic web connection (whether it is dial-up or broadband) and some that come with almost ostentatious portals, which can offer anything from cheap holidays and phone calls, all the way through to TV shows and radio stations.

While it might be unfair to focus on the most well known, there are a handful of ISPs that have worked hard to develop extensive music offerings. Among those are: AOL, Yahoo (which comes with BT Broadband), Tiscali, Blueyonder/NTL, Wannadoo (which will soon be renamed Orange after the mobile company bought it) and MSN.

As a subscriber to any of these services you will get access to their most exclusive packages, but even if you're not, it's still worth browsing around to see what they offer. Here's a small rundown of the benefits of each.

AOL UK

The AOL music service is divided up into various sections: a download shop, a video streaming service, the option to buy CD albums, various pre-programmed radio stations, access to Network Live concerts and webcasts.

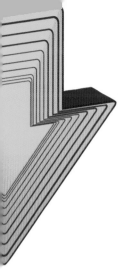

In terms of downloads, AOL UK is tied into iTunes, so if you're looking to download one of your favourite songs, or any track for that matter, you will be immediately redirected off to the iTunes music store. That's OK if you have iTunes and an iPod, but otherwise it's a pretty useless option.

AOL, however, has built its reputation on music webcasting and was the channel selected by organisers of the series of Live8 concerts to broadcast the event live on the web. Live footage from gigs has really become AOL's pièce de résistance.

What's more, there are other special details such as the option to buy sheet music for all of the featured artists and the opportunity to build online playlists. This is great if you are in earshot of your computer, but a bit annoying if not since they cannot be transferred on to a portable player.

AOL has also built in a particularly nice streaming service called 'CD Listening Party', where each week you get the chance to listen to tracks from 25 new albums and, from there, decide what you want to download. It's a great way to discover new music and add new stuff to your playlists.

AOL US
Music offerings on US ISPs are almost nonexistent apart from AOL, which has developed an extensive music site catering for almost any taste.

While it doesn't carry a full-on download shop, it does have a wide selection of free downloads - all available as Windows Media files, giving you the chance to sample new music with one click of the mouse.

But it doesn't stop there. AOL has gone to town in the US and the UK counterpart seems almost limited in comparison.

The video library is extensive, but you also have the option of streaming Network Live gigs, watching exclusive shows courtesy of AOL sessions, and listening to full-length albums in the 'AOL Listening Party' section. What's more, all of this is free to both subscribers and non-subscribers.

Small tip if you live outside the States: If you log on from a home computer, you will gain access to all of this. If you log on from a large company connection, however, it will recognise you are outside the States and immediately redirect you to your local AOL website. So, if you are at home, take advantage of the free downloads: it's a great way to access some fantastic American music.

Yahoo (available through BT Broadband UK, Yahoo UK and Europe, Yahoo US)

Instead of concentrating on downloads, Yahoo has a music product called Launch!

Launch almost completely concentrates on video and radio – but the videos cannot be transferred to a portable media player.

On the plus side, because it has invested so much into these areas it acts as a great way to discover music. The radio streaming service, for example, is one of the most popular on the web. One of its selling points is that you can customise your own radio stations. In the first instance, you select – by highlighting a tick box – your favourite genres and type in four of your preferred bands. From this, the Yahoo database will select which songs to fire out to you. If you like them, you can rate them highly and similar songs will be added to your station. If you don't like a particular song, it will delete that, plus others that sound like it, from your list.

The other highlight of Launch is its video service – the Yahoo service carries thousands and thousands of videos – bringing the equivalent of MTV straight to your PC.

However, the bottom line is, if you're looking for a download service, you're not going to find it here.

Tiscali (only available across Europe)

Tiscali has one of the most well-rounded music services on the web, complete with a download shop, video streaming, live concerts, plus specials such as the Tiscali Sessions.

Instead of attempting to build a download shop themselves, they employed the services of a company called OD2, who supply download stores to a variety of companies including MSN and Panasonic. The OD2-backed Tiscali store features 600,000 downloads.

The layout of Tiscali's music channel is very easy to navigate, and you don't need to subscribe to their internet package in order to access it. A special feature of Tiscali is SonicSelector – a place where you can store your downloads online, organise them, transfer them to a player and burn to CD. If you do burn your playlist or album to a CD, Tiscali also give you the very neat option of being able to design your very own CD cover – which isn't as easy as it sounds without a pre-designed template.

The other jewel in the Tiscali crown is its Sessions, where acts ranging from the established A-ha, and Echo and the Bunnymen through to newcomers Subways and Black Rebel Motorcycle Club have played small, intimate studio shows for exclusive streaming on Tiscali. To access this, you need to sign up beforehand.

Finally, if you are looking to discover new music, for a small amount each month, you can listen to any song in the Tiscali library – perfect if you are looking for new tracks to put on your playlists.

Blueyonder/NTL UK
Recently merged, the companies now offer the primary and best music service through NTL. The best all-round service is if you sign up to Broadband plus, which gives you access to Napster with a 40 per cent discount, MTV Live – for live gigs and artist interviews – Music Choice radio, VidZone (video-on-demand) and SonicSelector.

SonicSelector is exactly the same product offered by Tiscali, whereby download partner OD2 gives NTL/Blueyonder subscribers access to a library of 600,000 songs. However, on this ISP they are pitched at a slightly cheaper price. Files are available in the WMA format.

SonicSelector works in the same way: you can search for songs, organise your library online, build playlists and transfer and burn those songs to digital audio devices and CD. To buy music, NTL/Blueyonder redirects you out to HMV, which is a little odd given that their download store would be seen as competition.

Orange/Wanadoo Europe

Wanadoo has recently been bought by Orange, so if you are looking for music on that ISP, you will immediately be sent to the Orange music service, which operates with your home computer, as well as with your mobile phone.

MSN Music Club Worldwide

As part of Microsoft's ISP, unsurprisingly this is one of the largest download shops on the web. If you are signed up to get your net connection from MSN, then the store comes as part of that package. If you're not, you can still sign up separately. MSN carries one very special feature – aside from selling downloads, you can pay a monthly subscription fee which means you can listen to any song in their catalogue. It brings you your own personal jukebox straight to your home PC. Downloads from MSN are Windows Media format – obviously, since it's owned by Microsoft. All the downloads are transferable to virtually any player except for Sony and Apple products.

FUTURE
DEVELOPMENTS

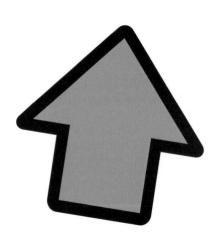

Streaming and portable services

For the past few years, the idea that music will be paid for like a utility – as in water or electricity – has been very much the talk of the music industry. It could be that we will pay a monthly rate and effectively 'rent' as much music as we like.

In fact, to some extent, this is already happening. Some services already offer online streaming for a fixed fee each month, whereby you can listen to anything in their library as much as you want.

Napster UK has the most pioneering offer on this front. As mentioned before, you can sign up to the Napster To Go service for a small fee each month and download as much music to both your PC and portable player as you like. If you stop paying, the music files automatically expire.

Rhapsody also has an enormous catalogue of music, and for a small monthly fixed price you are entitled to listen to that music from up to five PCs and transfer it to a portable device. It's not entirely different to Napster, but could offer up some sort of competition when it does arrive in Europe.

Essentially these are streaming services, where you don't actually own the music – and this could be one way the future of music lies.

Blogging

Blogging (taken from the term weblog) has become a phenomenon recently, although it is thought to have begun around ten years ago with a chap in the States who went under the alias Kibo and built a website to publish his online diary.

Blogging sites allow you to post an online diary, which more often than not will contain links to music, video clips, pictures and links out to other websites. It will also give other people the opportunity to post comments and thoughts about the stuff you have posted.

Blogging is a superb way to discover music. There are bound to be a whole host of people out there listening to music just like you, and a simple search for, say, a U2 blog, will lead you to what other music that person is listening to, and also the people who are responding to their blog.

To cope with the proliferation of weblogs on the internet, there are websites that have been set up as aggregators, which means they monitor the popularity of all the blogs registered with them and rank them accordingly. One of the best music blog aggregators is The Hype Machine: www.hype.non-standard.net. What's so special about The Hype Machine is that it lists the most popular MP3s on the blogs that have registered with it, and has created a daily chart of them, which you can listen to online. If you like a particular song, there will be a link direct to an online retailer.

There are millions of people posting blogs online every day containing an enormous amount of music – once you start, it's hard to know where to stop!

Networking Sites

These work in a similar way to blogs – more specifically, they even contain blogs. The most well-known networking site on the web at the moment is MySpace.

MySpace gives you a webpage and allows you to post a picture of yourself, plus other pictures on a separate page, list and detail your interests and make friends with other people on the network.

MySpace's draw is that it also gives musicians and bands the chance to build pages and post up to four songs for people to listen to, make part of their page (so, for example, if you are a big Madonna fan, you can go to her page and select a track which will then play whenever someone hits on your page), and download.

Naturally, there are many established artists on MySpace (www.myspace.com), and often you will not be able to download their songs for free. However, there are quite a few smaller and unsigned acts that do let you download certain tracks for free.

Meanwhile, every musician (or filmmaker, or artist) will have any number of friends signed up to their page, so it makes for great reading if you are on the hunt for new music. For example, you might log on to the White Stripes' page and find listed under their friends a whole host of bands you didn't know about – many of which could be giving away some of their music (all of it will normally be available as MP3). It's a great way to build new playlists, and if you really like a band, there will always be a link for you to go and buy their music, either digitally or on CD.

MySpace specialises in music, but it might also be worth checking out others such as Friendster, Bebo and HabboHotel, where people will often list the music they like. In the UK, there is also a new networking site set up called Bandwagon.co.uk, which essentially works in a similar way, but you can buy digital downloads straight from the site. However, you can only set up a page on Bandwagon.co.uk if you are a band or artist.

Downloading Straight From DAB Radio

There have been whispers about this for some time now – in fact, since the launch of DAB digital radio. Lots of us now own a digital radio and, once you've made that switch, you can never go back to tuning in your analogue FM station again.

It's also been said many times that it would be great if you were listening to a song you liked on the radio and, with one click of a button, you could download it to either your DAB Digital Radio, or your PC, or both.

Some radio companies have put money into trialling this, but as yet nothing concrete has come of it. However, that's only a matter of time. In the meantime, with some DAB radios you can control your listening as never before with functions that let you pause and rewind live radio, or, in some cases, record radio to an SD card. Your digital radio will need to have an SD-card slot in order for that to work.

Recently, the Digital Radio Development Bureau has also spoken about plans to introduce functions that would allow you to download the music you hear on the radio on your mobile phone, via a special DAB chip.

Legal Peer-to-peer Networks

There have been all manner of developments on this front, but so far the record labels have been reluctant to sign up, mainly because of fears that their music might be leaked on to the net for free.

There are many companies involved in making peer-to-peer work. In the UK, a company called Playlouder is developing a system where you will be able to sign up to their music-centric ISP, which will have a legalised P2P application within it. Similarly, in the US Mashboxx and Snocap are trying to develop legal alternatives. The idea is that all of those on the network will be able to share files with each other and, because those music files will be monitored, they will make sure that the record labels are paid for the songs people choose to download. That means you don't run the risk of getting sued. It also means you will be able to get your hands on as much music as you like by paying one monthly ISP charge.

Music Discovery Engines

These have been coming on to the market in the last couple of years and are a lot of fun. Two of the main music discovery engines on the web are Pandora and Lastfm.com.

How they work is pretty simple: you go to the website, create an account (this allows you also to create blogs, post pictures, create play-lists and share your playlists with other people who, in turn, will pass on details of their own), type in a list of your favourite bands and rank them accordingly.

In doing so, Pandora or Lastfm will chuck all that information through its database (which is compiled using information from other users' tastes and from its editors) and aim to throw back at you a whole list of bands and musicians who you may not have heard of, or had the time to listen to before.

You are given the option of listening to some tracks by that act and there are links for you to buy their music from online retailers. The most special feature about music discovery engines is that you can look at the lists of others who have similar music taste to your own – you never know what you might find.

Podcasting

Podcasting was one of the buzz words of 2005. Everyone seemed to be getting excited about them – and for good reason. A podcast (and yes, the word is a derivative play on the word iPod) is an MP3 you can subscribe to. When its creator updates it – usually on a weekly or monthly basis – your iPod, or digital audio device, will immediately download it (as long as it is hooked up to your computer).

However, at the moment, the music industry isn't too sure how they intend to license podcasts and so it is very rare to find a podcast with music on it.

When this situation clears up, which should be very soon, you will find that your favourite radio station will probably put together a podcast containing a whole array of songs. Chances are, too, your favourite artists might make special, exclusive podcasts. It will definitely prove to be one of the most exciting ways to download and discover music.

DOWNLOAD DICTIONARY –

SOME GENERAL TERMS USED IN THIS BOOK

3G The ultra-fast mobile network, soon to become standard. It enables fast transmission of information and the uploading of music and video files from the mobile networks.

À La Carte The purchasing of individual songs from online retailers.

AAC Apple's proprietary file-type format. CDs uploaded into iTunes will automatically be converted into AAC files, while songs purchased in iTunes will also be supplied as AAC and wrapped in Apple's Fairplay DRM.

AAC+ Another form of file-type format.

Adware Adware is software built into applications and software that can be downloaded from the net. It is a way for the creator of the software to reclaim costs, by building in advertising. Providing it isn't too intrusive, it can work quite effectively, but has developed a bad reputation since it can often crash or corrupt computers.

ATRAC3 Sony's proprietary file-type format. Files transferred from a computer to a Sony device via the company's software will automatically be converted into ATRAC3.

Autofill This is a function within iTunes that works with the company's Shuffle flash device. By hitting on the 'autofill' button a number of songs from your library will be randomly selected and instantly transferred to the Shuffle.

Blog/Blogging A function that allows you to post information on to the web. Blog sites will give you a page on the internet which you can personalise. People use blogs to keep online journals, post images, music and film and effectively share them with their friends.

Bluetooth An internal piece of technology on a variety of devices, from mobiles through to computers. It allows users within 100m of each other to swap files.

Broadband The connection from your computer to the web. Broadband is ultra fast and large and therefore makes downloading a lot easier. It's also switched on all the time, so access to it is immediate.

Burning The copying of music and film files from your hard drive to a CD slotted into your CD drive.

Bytes A byte is a unit of storage measurement in computers, regardless of the type of data being stored. Megabytes are literally millions of bytes, while gigabytes are billions of bytes.

Caller Tunes/Ringback Tones A ringtone someone hears when they call your phone, instead of the normal dialling tone.

Copyright Infringement The sharing and using of unlicensed music files on the web is one form of copyright infringement and is illegal.

DAB Radio Digital (as opposed to analogue) radio, which, as well as transmitting through the air, also uses the web to transmit broadcasts, data and information.

Data Charge This will be a charge added to the cost of your 'over the air' download from the network company. While you are charged for the file you have purchased, you will also be charged for it to be sent to your phone over the mobile network.

Data Compression Data compression is the process whereby digital files are reduced in size in order to make them less bulky to store on your hard drive and easier and faster to transfer. Uncompressed files would take up an enormous amount of space on the memory of a computer. By ripping your music into a software application such as Windows Media, you will automatically be compressing your songs.

Data Transmission The transmission of information over the web or mobile networks.

Dial-up A smaller, more limited web network that requires your computer to dial-in in order to get access. Downloading is very laborious and slow on dial-up connections.

Digital Audio Player A digital audio player is a piece of hardware that carries a memory and also acts as a music player, complete with control functions: play, rewind, fast-forward, etc. The most well-known digital audio player is the iPod.

Digitise To digitise anything means taking the original copy of something – a song on a CD or a photograph – and either loading it or scanning it into your computer. During this process, you will be effectively digitising your collections.

Docking Port The slot in your portable device that allows you to hook it up to a computer via a USB cable.

Downloads The process of obtaining files – whether they are music, video, images or even PDFs and word documents from email accounts or websites – and transferring them to your computer's hard drive.

DRDB The Digital Radio Development Bureau.

DRM DRM stands for Digital Rights Management. It is a piece of embedded technology that controls the way in which you can use a digital file. For example, if you buy a song from iTunes, Apple's DRM will allow you to transfer only that song to an iPod, burn it to CD a limited amount of times and play it on a limited number of computers.

Fairplay DRM Fairplay is the digital rights management application used by Apple to limit your usage of any file purchased from iTunes.

Flash Memory Card A flash memory card is a small card that can be slotted into a digital audio device or a mobile phone, which carries a small memory and can therefore hold a certain amount of data. Normal sizes include 128MB, 256MB and 512MB.

Flash Player A flash player contains a flash memory – unlike a hard disk, this can be erased and written over time and time again. Often flash players will have smaller memories, compared with standard digital audio players, but this is set to change.

Hard Drive The hard drive is the part of the computer that contains all of its memory, its software applications and stores of all your files.

HSDPA Standing for High Speed Downlink Packet Access, this is the next generation for mobile networks – it's faster than 3G and is particularly useful for the transmission of film and TV shows, as moving pictures and sound can easily be sent over the network.

Internet Service Provider A company that supplies internet connections and online information services.

IP address Every computer will have an address if it is hooked up to the internet – known as its IP.

iTunes Apple's iTunes comprises the iTunes music store and its music player software, which, like its competitors, allows you to rip, burn, organise and listen to your music collection. It works seamlessly with the iPod, but doesn't work with any other digital audio devices.

Memory Stick/Card A little chip that carries a small amount of memory: normally 512MB. A memory stick – or a USB drive – is like a small key upon which files can be transferred. A memory card gives mobile devices – such as digital audio players, cameras and mobiles extra memory.

MMS Multimedia messaging – this is the function that will allow you to send a music, film or photo file over your mobile network to another mobile phone or email account.

Mobile 'hot key' One button on your phone that, with one click, will give you access to a mobile network's music, film, or even sport and news offerings.

MP3 A compressed music file type. It is the most popular on the web and comes without any DRM restrictions.

Networking Sites An online web network that connects friends through their online pages.

OMA DRM OMA is the digital rights management application used by the mobile networks – it limits your usage of any music file purchased directly from the networks.

P2P/Peer-to-peer/File Sharing The sharing of files between users on the net via software 'clients' available as free downloads on the web.

Podcast The timed delivery of a programme – usually comprised of speech – which is downloaded via a system called RSS. Those signed up to podcasts will have them automatically sent to a digital audio device when it is synched with a nominated computer.

Polyphonic Tones Instead of a monotone, synthesised sound, a polyphonic ringtone is made up of a number of layers, making it sound more like the original piece of music.

Posting The term that describes uploading text and files on to web pages.

PSP The Sony PlayStation Portable: a multi-enabled device for gaming and music that also connects wirelessly to the internet.

RealPlayer The proprietary software owned by RealMusic, which has been adopted by various mobile companies and is available as a free download on the web. It allows you to rip, burn, organise and listen to your music collection, while supplying other functions such as at least 22 pre-programmed radio stations and information on bands and artists.

Realtones General term for ringtones that sound almost identical to the original piece of music.

Ringtones Short snippets of music used on mobile phones to signal an incoming call.

Ripping Ripping is the process whereby you take your CDs, insert them into your hard drive and copy them to the memory of your computer. Depending on which music software you use, they will then show up in the Media Library and also on your local drive (which is normally 'My Music' on the local C drive if you're using a PC).

Set-top Box The device that sits on top of a TV and receives trans-missions and data.

Side-loading The process by which you can upload music files to your phone without having to download them from the web. Side-loading involves you attaching a type of firewire cable (which will come with your phone) to your computer. Files from your computer can then be transferred using applications such as Windows Media Player or, more often, software supplied with the mobile phone.

Software Application A software application is essentially the piece of kit that allows you to perform functions on your computer – Microsoft's suite of software applications includes Microsoft Word, Excel and so forth. When it comes to downloading, anything from iTunes, Windows Media Player, and RealPlayer can be described as soft-ware applications.

Sony SonicStage Sony's proprietary software that manages the conversion and transfer of music files to its devices.

Spyware Spyware is a type of software that watches what users do with their computers while online and sends this information to hackers. Spyware can collect many different types of information about a user, even information typed in, such as bank details. It is often built into downloadable applications available for free on the net, so it is wise not to download anything which is not considered legitimate.

Streaming The transmission of music and video over the web that allows you to tune in and listen, but not retain the file.

Sync Wizard The procedure your computer will go through when you plug in your digital audio device for the first time. It will acknowledge that the device is there, ask you what kind of device it is (normally from a menu of options) and open a gateway so the computer and device can effectively 'talk' to each other.

Trutones A ringtone that is an actual edit of a piece of music. Instead of hearing a synthesised copy, you will actually hear a clip of your chosen piece of music.

USB cable A USB cable links external memory drives (such as digital audio players) to your computer's hard drive. Most computers come with four different USB ports, allowing you to plug in four different types of devices at a time.

WAP Portal Effectively a mini-website accessible on your mobile phone.

WAV A larger file type than an MP3, and generally considered to be better quality.

Webcasting A live transmission of an event over the web. Webcasts can be viewed on a variety of websites.

Windows Media Player Microsoft's proprietary software, which comes automatically installed with all PCs. It allows you to rip, burn, organise and listen to your music collection, and is compatible with all digital audio devices except the iPod.

WMA Microsoft's proprietary file format. CDs ripped and uploaded into Windows Media Player, as well as many files purchased on the web, are encoded in this format.

PLAYLISTS

Here are some playlists to get you started. Of course you can add to them and adapt them to your own taste as much as you like.

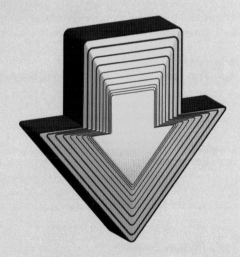

PUNK

Smash It Up...

1 **THE CLASH**
Complete Control

2 **SEX PISTOLS**
God Save The Queen

3 **THE RAMONES**
Beat On The Brat

4 **X-RAY SPEX**
The Day The World Turned Day-Glo

5 **HEARTBREAKERS**
Chinese Rocks

6 **THE DAMNED**
Smash It Up

7 **GENERATION X**
Valley Of The Dolls

8 **SIOUXSIE & THE BANSHEES**
Jigsaw Feeling

9 THE STRANGLERS
(Get A) Grip (On Yourself)

10 SHAM 69
Borstal Breakout

11 BLONDIE
Rip Her To Shreds

12 THE SLITS
Typical Girls

13 RICHARD HELL
Blank Generation

14 SEX PISTOLS / SID VICIOUS
Something Else

15 BUZZCOCKS
What Do I Get

16 THE JAM
In The City

17 PUBLIC IMAGE LTD
Public Image

ROADTRIP

Go Your Own Way...

1 **TOM PETTY & THE HEARTBREAKERS**
American Girl

2 **CANNED HEAT**
On The Road Again

3 **BRUCE SPRINGSTEEN**
Thunder Road

4 **CYNDI LAUPER**
I Drove All Night

5 **AMERICA**
Ventura Highway

6 **THE CARS**
My Best Friend's Girl

7 **DON HENLEY**
Boys Of Summer

8 **FLEETWOOD MAC**
Go Your Own Way

9 STEPPENWOLF
Born To Be Wild

10 CREEDENCE CLEARWATER REVIVAL
Proud Mary

11 CREAM
Badge

12 WILLIE NELSON
On The Road Again

13 AC/DC
Highway To Hell

14 ERIC CLAPTON
Cocaine

15 ELTON JOHN
Philadelphia Freedom

16 THE GO GOS
Vacation

17 ELVIS PRESLEY
Viva Las Vegas

BREAKUP

Dry Your Eyes...

1 **McALMONT & BUTLER**
Yes

2 **BEN FOLDS FIVE**
Song For The Dumped

3 **THE KINKS**
Days

4 **DIANA ROSS**
Remember Me

5 **KELIS**
Caught Out There

6 **THE STREETS**
Dry Your Eyes

7 **10CC**
I'm Not In Love

8 **GEORGE MICHAEL**
Careless Whisper

GOT IT COVERED

Comfortably Numb...

1 JOHNNY CASH
Hurt (Nine Inch Nails)

2 R.E.M
Strange (Wire)

3 THE JAM
David Watts (The Kinks)

4 SID VICIOUS
My Way (Frank Sinatra)

5 LULU
The Man Who Sold The World (David Bowie)

6 DAVID BOWIE
China Girl (Iggy Pop)

7 KIRSTY MACOLL
A New England (Billy Bragg)

8 THE FUTUREHEADS
Hounds Of Love (Kate Bush)

9 THE BYRDS
Mr Tambourine Man (Bob Dylan)

10 FLYING LIZARDS
Money (Berry Gordy/The Beatles)

11 THE SLITS
I Heard It Through The Grapevine (Marvin Gaye)

12 SCISSOR SISTERS
Comfortably Numb (Pink Floyd)

13 SIOUXSIE & THE BANSHEES
Dear Prudence (The Beatles)

14 THE FALL
There's A Ghost In My House (R Dean Taylor)

15 PET SHOP BOYS
Always On My Mind (Elvis Presley)

16 HAPPY MONDAYS
Step On (John Kongos)

17 RED HOT CHILI PEPPERS
Higher Ground (Stevie Wonder)

SCOTTISH ROCK

Kiss This Thing Goodbye...

1 AZTEC CAMERA
Oblivious

2 THE SKIDS
Into The Valley

3 PRIMAL SCREAM
Come Together

4 THE JESUS & MARY CHAIN
Reverence

5 DEACON BLUE
Real Gone Kid

6 SIMPLE MINDS
Love Song

7 ORANGE JUICE
Rip It Up

8 ARAB STRAP
Here We Go

THE STONES

Start Me Up...

1 It's All Over Now

2 The Last Time

3 (I Can't Get No) Satisfaction

4 19th Nervous Breakdown

5 Have You Seen Your Mother, Baby, Standing In The Shadow?

6 We Love You

7 Jumpin' Jack Flash

8 Honky Tonk Women

BEATLES

I Want To Tell You...

SOUNDTRACK

Stuck In The Middle With You...

1 ELTON JOHN
Tiny Dancer (Almost Famous)

2 IGGY POP
Lust For Life (Trainspotting)

3 THE DOORS
The End (Apocalypse Now)

4 AIMEE MANN
Save Me (Magnolia)

5 THE PSYCHEDELIC FURS
Pretty In Pink (Pretty In Pink)

6 STEALERS WHEEL
Stuck In The Middle With You (Reservoir Dogs)

7 FRANKIE VALLI
Grease Is The Word (Grease)

8 NILSSON
Everybody's Talkin' (Midnight Cowboy)

18 **HARRY BELAFONTE**
Jump In Line /Shake Shake Senora (Beetlejuice)

19 **SIMPLE MINDS**
Don't You (Forget About Me) (Breakfast Club)

20 **JIMMY CLIFF**
The Harder They Come (The Harder They Come)

21 **ISAAC HAYES**
Theme From Shaft (Shaft)

22 **JACK WILD, SHANI WALLIS etc**
I'd Do Anything (Oliver!)

23 **PHOENIX**
Too Young (Lost In Translation)

24 **NANCY SINATRA**
Bang Bang, (My Baby Shot Me Down) (Kill Bill Vol 1)

25 **WINGS**
Live And Let Die (Live And Let Die)

AIR GUITAR

Are You Experienced?...

1. **BAD COMPANY**
   Feel Like Makin' Love

2. **DEEP PURPLE**
   Smoke On The Water

3. **THE EAGLES**
   Life In The Fast Lane

4. **ZZ TOP**
   Sharp Dressed Man

5. **THE HIVES**
   Hate To Say I Told You So

6. **THE WHITE STRIPES**
   Seven Nation Army

7. **BOSTON**
   More Than A Feeling

8. **ARGENT**
   Hold Your Head Up

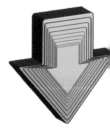

9 JIMI HENDRIX
Are You Experienced?

10 LED ZEPPELIN
Black Dog

11 THE GUESS WHO
American Woman

12 FREE
Wishing Well

13 THE UNDERTONES
Teenage Kicks

14 THE KINKS
You Really Got Me

15 BLUE OYSTER CULT
(Don't Fear) The Reaper

16 DAVID BOWIE
Jean Genie

17 THE YARDBIRDS
Over Under Sideways Down

BRITPOP

Common People...

1 **BLUR**
For Tomorrow

2 **SUEDE**
Animal Nitrate

3 **PULP**
Mis-Shapes

4 **ELASTICA**
Connection

5 **MENSWEAR**
Daydreamer

6 **OASIS**
Supersonic

7 **THE BLUETONES**
Are You Blue Or Are You Blind?

8 **SUPERGRASS**
Alright

ROMANCE

Dream A Little Dream...

1 JOAN ARMATRADING
Love & Affection

2 THE SYLISTICS
You Make Me Feel Brand New

3 PAUL WELLER
You Do Something To Me

4 THE BEATLES
Something

5 BOB DYLAN
I Want You

6 AZTEC CAMERA
We Could Send Letters

7 LONGPIGS
On And On

8 ROBERTA FLACK
The First Time Ever I Saw Your Face

50s/ROCK 'N' ROLL

All Shook Up...

1 BILL HALEY & THE COMETS
Rock Around The Clock

2 JERRY LEE LEWIS
Whole Lotta Shakin' Going On

3 CLIFF RICHARD
Move It

4 BUDDY HOLLY
Rave On

5 JOHNNY CASH & THE TENNESSEE TWO
I Walk The Line

6 FRANKIE LYMON & THE TEENAGERS
Why Do Fools Fall In Love

7 FATS DOMINO
Blueberry Hill

8 HANK WILLIAMS
Honky Tonk Blues

60s

Whole Lotta Love...

1 **THE BONZO DOG DOO-DAH BAND**
I'm The Urban Spaceman

2 **THE MONKEES**
Last Train To Clarksville

3 **BILLY FURY**
It's Only Make Believe

4 **THE SMALL FACES**
Itchycoo Park

5 **THE VELVET UNDERGROUND**
Venus In Furs

6 **CREATION**
How Does It Feel To Feel

7 **TOM JONES**
Help Yourself

8 **LOVE**
Alone Again Or

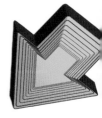

9 GARY PUCKETT & THE UNION GAP
Young Girl

10 TOMMY ROE
Dizzy

11 THE MAMAS & THE PAPAS
California Dreamin'

12 DONOVAN
Sunshine Superman

13 THE LOVIN' SPOONFUL
Do You Believe In Magic

14 THE MOODY BLUES
Nights In White Satin

15 PINK FLOYD
Lucifer Sam

16 THE TEMPTATIONS
Ball Of Confusion

17 CARLA THOMAS
B.A.B.Y

18 THE BOX TOPS
The Letter

19 DUSTY SPRINGFIELD
You Don't Have To Say You Love Me

20 THE BEACH BOYS
Wouldn't It Be Nice

21 THE YARDBIRDS
Heart Full Of Soul

22 LED ZEPPELIN
Whole Lotta Love

23 COUNTRY JOE & THE FISH
The Fish Cheer/I Feel Like I'm Fixin' To Die Rag

24 THE MOVE
Blackberry Way

25 SIMON & GARFUNKEL
Homeward Bound

70s

Anarchy In The UK...

1 **THE CLASH**
White Man In Hammersmith Palais

2 **LENE LOVICH**
Lucky Number

3 **MAXINE NIGHTINGALE**
Right Back Where We Started From

4 **DR HOOK**
Sylvia's Mother

5 **QUEEN**
We Are The Champions

6 **IAN DURY & THE BLOCKHEADS**
Hit Me With Your Rhythm Stick

7 **PINK FLOYD**
Money

8 **GEORGE HARRISON**
My Sweet Lord

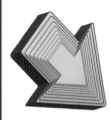

80s

Same Old Scene...

1 SOFT CELL
Tainted Love

2 ABC
All Of My Heart

3 GO GO'S
Our Lips Are Sealed

4 MADNESS
Our House

5 THE SPECIALS
Ghost Town

6 ROXY MUSIC
Same Old Scene

7 S-XPRESS
Theme From S-Express

8 JAPAN
Quiet Life

90s

Smells Like Teen Spirit...

1 **THE VERVE**
Bittersweet Symphony

2 **THE CHEMICAL BROTHERS**
Block Rockin' Beats

3 **U2**
Mysterious Ways

4 **THE STEREOPHONICS**
Local Boy In The Photograph

5 **ALL SAINTS**
Pure Shores

6 **LUSH**
Sweetness & Light

7 **MANIC STREET PREACHERS**
You Love Us

8 **KYLIE MINOGUE**
Confide In Me

DISCO

Don't Stop The Music...

1 **CROWN HEIGHTS AFFAIR**
You Gave Me Love

2 **TINA CHARLES**
I Love To Love

3 **THE TRAMMPS**
Disco Inferno

4 **BEE GEES**
You Should Be Dancing

5 **DONNA SUMMER**
I Feel Love

6 **SHANNON**
Let The Music Play

7 **SHEILA B DEVOTION**
Spacer

8 **GIBSON BROTHERS**
Cuba

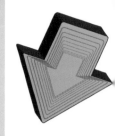

DIVAS

Bootylicious...

1. **DIANA ROSS**
   I'm Still Waiting

2. **SADE**
   Hang On To Your Love

3. **GOLDFRAPP**
   Strict Machine

4. **TINA TURNER**
   We Don't Need Another Hero

5. **GRACE JONES**
   Pull Up To The Bumper

6. **CHER**
   Gypsies, Tramps & Thieves

7. **WHITNEY HOUSTON**
   How Will I Know?

8. **JANET JACKSON**
   When I Think Of You

BOYBAND

I Wanna Sex You Up...

1 **TAKE THAT**
Back For Good

2 **NEW KIDS ON THE BLOCK**
You Got It (The Right Stuff)

3 **BOYZONE**
Father & Son

4 **THE MONKEES**
Daydream Believer

5 **FIVE**
Keep On Movin'

6 **BLUE**
Fly By II

7 **EAST 17**
House Of Love

8 **NSYNC**
I Want You Back

DUETS

Back Together Again...

1 KENNY ROGERS AND DOLLY PARTON
Islands In The Stream

2 ISOBEL CAMPBELL & MARK LANEGAN
Ramblin' Man

3 PRINCE & SHEENA EASTON
U Got The Look

4 BARBRA STREISAND & BARRY GIBB
Guilty

5 ELTON JOHN & KIKI DEE
Don't Go Breaking My Heart

6 SONY & CHER
I Got You Babe

7 TEXAS & PAUL BUCHANAN
Getaway

8 MARVIN GAYE & TAMMI TERRELL
Ain't No Mountain High Enough

GOTH ROCK

The Beautiful People...

1 **THE CULT**
Resurrection Joe

2 **THE MARCH VIOLETS**
Snake Dance

3 **THE SISTERS OF MERCY**
This Corrosion

4 **MARILYN MANSON**
The Beautiful People

5 **KILLING JOKE**
Love Like Blood

6 **THE CURE**
A Forest

7 **THE ICARUS LINE**
Party The Baby Off

8 **SIOUXSIE & THE BANSHEES**
Night Shift

FATHER'S DAY

Daddy Cool...

1. **OASIS**
Rock 'n' Roll Star

2. **SLADE**
Cum On Feel The Noize

3. **HARD FI**
Hard To Beat

4. **GENESIS**
Abacab

5. **THE WHO**
Substitute

6. **PEARL JAM**
Alive

7. **OCEAN COLOUR SCENE**
The Riverboat Song

8. **PAUL WELLER**
The Changing Man

HIP HOP

Gangsta's Paradise...

1 THE SUGARHILL GANG
Rapper's Delight

2 GRANDMASTER FLASH AND THE FURIOUS FIVE
The Message

3 AFRIKA BAMBAATAA AND THE SOULSONIC
FORCE
Planet Rock

4 KURTIS BLOW
The Breaks

5 ERIC B. AND RAKIM
Paid In Full

6 THE 45 KING
The 900 Number

7 PUBLIC ENEMY
Don't Believe The Hype

8 QUEEN LATIFAH
Ladies First

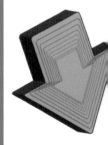

RAP

Insane In The Brain...

1. **GRANDMASTER FLASH AND MELLE MEL**
   White Lines (Don't Do It)

2. **KRS ONE**
   Sound Of Da Police

3. **PUBLIC ENEMY**
   Fight The Power

4. **NAUGHTY BY NATURE**
   OPP

5. **NWA**
   Straight Outta Compton

6. **THE GETO BOYS**
   Bring It On

7. **CYPRESS HILL**
   Insane In The Brain

8. **BRAND NUBIAN**
   Brand Nubian

HEAVY METAL

Welcome To The Jungle...

1 IRON MAIDEN
Run To The Hills

2 ALICE COOPER
Elected

3 THE CULT
Love Removal Machine

4 VAN HALEN
Why Can't This Be Love?

5 BLACK SABBATH
War Pigs

6 MOTLEY CRUE
Girls Girls Girls

7 LED ZEPPELIN
Immigrant Song

8 JUDAS PRIEST
Breaking The Law

18 AC/DC
Back In Black

19 NAZARETH
Bad Bad Boy

20 METALLICA
Enter Sandman

21 OZZY OSBOURNE
Bark At The Moon

22 SAXON
747 (Strangers In The Night)

23 UFO
Doctor Doctor

24 METALLICA
One

25 SPINAL TAP
Big Bottom

CLASSICAL

Land Of Hope And Glory...

1 **COPLAND**
Fanfare For The Common Man

2 **ROSSINI**
Overture From William Tell

3 **WAGNER**
Ride Of The Valkyries

4 **TCHAIKOVSKY**
Russian Dance From 'Nutcracker'

5 **DUKAS**
The Sorcerer's Apprentice

6 **MOZART**
Eine Kleine Nachtmusik

7 **MENDELSSOHN**
Overture From 'Fingal's Cave'

8 **BACH**
Toccata And Fugue

18 BEETHOVEN
Symphony No. 5 - Allegro Con Brio

19 TCHAIKOVSKY
1812 Overture

20 MOZART
Overture From 'The Marriage Of Figaro'

21 VIVALDI
Spring From 'The Four Seasons'

22 BIZET
Marche Du Toreador From 'Carmen'

23 HOLST
Mars From 'The Planets'

24 RAVEL
Bolero

25 TCHAIKOVSKY
Swan Lake Highlights

SEDUCTION

Close The Door...

1. **INXS**
   Need You Tonight

2. **MADONNA**
   Justify Your Love

3. **LIBERTY X**
   Just A Little

4. **DONNA SUMMER**
   Down Deep Inside

5. **AIR**
   Sexy Boy

6. **KYLIE MINOGUE**
   Slow

7. **DURAN DURAN**
   The Chauffeur

8. **MASSIVE ATTACK**
   Protection

CHILDREN'S

If You're Happy And You Know It...

RELAXATION

Enjoy The Silence...

1 **CORINNE BAILEY RAE**
Like A Star

2 **KATE BUSH**
Breathing

3 **MORCHEEBA**
Blindfold

4 **NOUVELLE VAGUE**
I Melt With You

5 **PHOENIX**
Run Run Run

6 **ZERO 7**
I Have Seen

7 **AIR**
Kelly Watch The Stars

8 **DUBSTAR**
Stars

BURT BACHARACH

Magic Moments...

1 **THE CARPENTERS**
Close To You

2 **DUSTY SPRINGFIELD**
The Look Of Love

3 **ANNE MURRAY**
I'll Never Fall In Love Again

4 **JACKIE DESHANNON**
What The World Needs Now Is Love

5 **PERRY COMO**
Magic Moments

6 **DIONNE WARWICK**
Walk On By

7 **CILLA BLACK**
Anyone Who Had A Heart

8 **DIONNE WARWICK**
Do You Know The Way To San Jose?

MOTHER'S DAY

Never Forget...

1 ROBBIE WILLIAMS
Angels

2 ANASTACIA
I'm Outta Love

3 ROY ORBISON
Pretty Woman

4 SIMPLY RED
A New Flame

5 BILL WITHERS
Lovely Day

6 GEORGE MICHAEL
Cowboys & Angels

7 BILLY JOEL
Just The Way You Are

8 COLDPLAY
Clocks

CHRISTMAS

Santa Claus Is Back In Town...

1 THE WAITRESSES
Christmas Wrapping

2 SLADE
Merry Xmas Everybody

3 THE CARPENTERS
Merry Christmas Darling

4 LOW
Just Like Christmas

5 GREG LAKE
I Believe In Father Christmas

6 THE SUPREMES
Santa Claus Is Coming To Town

7 JONA LEWIE
Stop The Cavalry

8 BING CROSBY & DAVID BOWIE
Little Drummer Boy

GLAM ROCK

Killer Queen...

1 **SWEET**
Ballroom Blitz

2 **T. REX**
Metal Guru

3 **MOTT THE HOOPLE**
Roll Away The Stone

4 **THE FACES**
Stay With Me

5 **SPARKS**
This Town Ain't Big Enough For Both Of Us

6 **MUD**
Dynamite

7 **THE GLITTER BAND**
Angel Face

8 **HELLO**
New York Groove

18 **CHRIS SPEDDING**
Motorbikin'

19 **T. REX**
Children Of The Revolution

20 **SLADE**
Skweeze Me Pleeze Me

21 **WIZZARD**
Angel Fingers

22 **GOLDEN EARRING**
Radar Love

23 **SUZI QUATRO**
Devil Gate Drive

24 **SPARKS**
Amateur Hour

25 **NEW YORK DOLLS**
Jet Boy

WORKOUT

Time To Burn...

1 LIVIN' JOY
Dreamer (Radio Mix)

2 BASEMENT JAXX
Flylife

3 ULTRA NATE
Free (Radio Edit)

4 ADAMSKI
Killer (Album Version)

5 DAVID MORALES & THE BAD YARD CLUB
FEAT. CRYSTAL WATERS **In De Ghetto**

6 MY FRIEND SAM FEATURING VIOLA WILLS
It's My Pleasure

7 CE CE PENISTON
Finally

8 HAPPY CLAPPERS
I Believe

INDIE

Cut Your Hair...

1. **BLOC PARTY**
   Helicopter

2. **BRENDAN BENSON**
   Cold Hands Warm Heart

3. **THE ARCADE FIRE**
   Lies

4. **GRANDADDY**
   The Crystal Lake

5. **THE WEDDING PRESENT**
   Brassneck

6. **THE RACONTEURS**
   Steady As She Goes

7. **BELLE & SEBASTIAN**
   Legal Man

8. **MERCURY REV**
   Opus 40

MOTOWN

Got To Be There...

1 THE VELVELETTES
Needle In A Haystack

2 MARVIN GAYE
I Heard It Through The Grapevine

3 THE JACKSONS
ABC

4 STEVIE WONDER
For Once In My Life

5 THE FOUR TOPS
Bernadette

6 THE SUPREMES
Baby Love

7 THE TEMPTATIONS
Just My Imagination (Running Away With Me)

8 SMOKEY ROBINSON & THE MIRACLES
Going To A Go Go

MUSICALS

Send In The Clowns...

1 *OLIVER!*
It's A Fine Life

2 *BUGSY MALONE*
You Give A Little Love

3 *GREASE*
Summer Nights

4 *OKLAHOMA!*
Oh, What A Beautiful Morning

5 *SOUTH PACIFIC*
I'm Gonna Wash That Man Right Outta My Hair

6 *CHITTY CHITTY BANG BANG*
Hushabye Mountain

7 *KISS ME, KATE*
Too Darn Hot

8 *THE SOUND OF MUSIC*
My Favourite Things

CHILL-OUT

Peace...

1 **THE BEACH BOYS**
Feel Flows

2 **HERB ALPERT**
Rotation

3 **MANUEL GOTTSCHING**
E2-E4

4 **DOUBLE**
The Captain Of Her Heart

5 **KOOL AND THE GANG**
Summer Madness

6 **GROOVE ARMADA**
At The River

7 **LAMBCHOP**
Up With People (Zero 7 Mix)

8 **NIGHTMARES ON WAX**
Nights Interlude

HOLIDAY

Feeling Hot Hot Hot...

1. **CLIFF RICHARD**
   Summer Holiday

2. **MADONNA**
   Holiday

3. **IAN DURY & THE BLOCKHEADS**
   Reasons To Be Cheerful Part 3

4. **WHIGFIELD**
   Saturday Night

5. **DJ JAZZY JEFF & THE FRESH PRINCE**
   Summertime

6. **THE ISLEY BROTHERS**
   Summer Breeze

7. **THE LOVIN' SPOONFUL**
   Summer In The City

8. **THE DANDY WARHOLS**
   Every Day Should Be A Holiday

CROONERS PAST & PRESENT

Let There Be Love...

1. **FRANK SINATRA**
   My Kind Of Town

2. **TONY BENNETT**
   The Lady Is A Tramp

3. **DEAN MARTIN**
   Volare

4. **FRANK SINATRA**
   Strangers In The Night

5. **BING CROSBY**
   Swinging On A Star

6. **PERRY COMO**
   Some Enchanted Evening

7. **TONY BENNETT**
   I Left My Heart In San Francisco

8. **SAMMY DAVIS JUNIOR**
   Mr Bojangles

REGGAE

Everything Is Great...

1 **BOB MARLEY & THE WAILERS**
Could You Be Loved

2 **SHAGGY**
Oh Carolina

3 **JOHNNY NASH**
I Can See Clearly Now

4 **KEN BOOTHE**
Everything I Own

5 **INI KAMOZE**
Here Comes The Hotstepper

6 **DESMOND DEKKER**
Israelites

7 **MUSICAL YOUTH**
Pass The Dutchie

8 **DILLINGER**
Cocaine In My Brain

9 SUGAR MINOTT
Good Thing Going

10 SEAN PAUL
Get Busy

11 INNER CIRCLE
Everything Is Great

12 BLACK UHURU
What Is Life?

13 DENNIS BROWN
Money In My Pocket

14 NICKY THOMAS
Love Of The Common People

15 SLY & ROBBIE
Night Nurse

16 DAVE & ANSELL COLLINS
Double Barrel

17 ALTHEA & DONNA
Uptown Top Ranking

JAZZ

Strange Fruit...

1. **YUSEF LATEEF**
   Love Theme From Spartacus

2. **BILLIE HOLIDAY**
   Strange Fruit

3. **PHAROAH SANDERS**
   You've Got To Have Freedom

4. **NINA SIMONE**
   Baltimore

5. **MONGO SANTAMARIA**
   Afro Blue

6. **MILES DAVIS**
   All Blues

7. **JOHN COLTRANE**
   Alabama

8. **THELONIOUS MONK**
   Epistrophy

FOLK

Go Your Way...

1. **BOB DYLAN**
Knockin' On Heaven's Door

2. **DAVEY GRAHAM**
Angi

3. **JONI MITCHELL**
Blue

4. **JACKSON C FRANK**
Blues Run The Game

5. **FAIRPORT CONVENTION**
Who Knows Where The Time Goes

6. **BERT JANSCH**
Poison

7. **NEIL YOUNG**
Comes A Time

8. **DONOVAN**
Wear Your Love Like Heaven

OLD SCHOOL R&B

Mess Around...

1. **FATS DOMINO**
   I Hear You Knocking

2. **BIG MAMA THORNTON**
   Hound Dog

3. **ERNIE K-DOE**
   Mother-In-Law

4. **RUFUS THOMAS**
   Walking The Dog

5. **WILSON PICKETT**
   Mustang Sally

6. **ETTA JAMES**
   Fire

7. **BIG JOE TURNER**
   Shake Rattle & Roll

8. **LITTLE RICHARD**
   Lucille

SOUL

Try A Little Tenderness...

1 **AL GREEN**
Love & Happiness

2 **SAM COOKE**
You Send Me

3 **ARETHA FRANKLIN**
Don't Play That Song

4 **PERCY SLEDGE**
When A Man Loves A Woman

5 **OTIS REDDING**
Try A Little Tenderness

6 **IRMA THOMAS**
It's Raining

7 **CLARENCE CARTER**
Patches

8 **CANDI STATON**
I'd Rather Be An Old Man's Sweetheart

9 SAM & DAVE
Hold On I'm Coming

10 IKE & TINA TURNER
River Deep Mountain High

11 JOHNNIE TAYLOR
Who's Making Love?

12 OTIS CLAY
Trying To Live My Life Without You

13 WILLIAM BELL & JUDY CLAY
Private Number

14 FREDA PAYNE
Band Of Gold

15 THE SHANGRI-LAS
Leader Of The Pack

16 SMOKEY ROBINSON & THE MIRACLES
More Love

17 MARLENA SHAW
California Soul

COUNTRY

Rollin' With The Flow...

1. HANK WILLIAMS
Lovesick Blues

2. LEFTY FRIZZELL
Look What Thoughts Will Do

3. BOB WILLS & HIS TEXAS PLAYBOYS
Take Me Back To Tulsa

4. ERNEST TUBB
Walking The Floor Over You

5. THE LOUVIN BROTHERS
I Don't Believe You've Met My Baby

6. ROY ACUFF
Blue Eyes Crying In The Rain

7. PATSY CLINE
Crazy

8. JIMMIE RODGERS
Blue Yodel No. 1 (T For Texas)

SURFING

Wipeout...

1. **THE BEACH BOYS**
   Surfin' USA

2. **THE BEACH BOYS**
   California Girls

3. **THE BEACH BOYS**
   Surfin'

4. **THE BEACH BOYS**
   Girls On The Beach

5. **JAN & DEAN**
   Ride The Wild Surf

6. **JAN & DEAN**
   Summer Means Fun

7. **JAN & DEAN**
   Sidewalk Surfin'

8. **THE TORNADOES**
   Bustin' Surfboards

GARAGE

Gotta Get Thru This...

1 THE ARTFUL DODGER FEAT. CRAIG DAVID
Re-Rewind

2 TINA MOORE
Never Gonna Let You Go

3 SNEAKER PIMPS
Spin Spin Sugar (Armands Dark Garage Mix)

4 WOOKIE
Scrappy

5 THE STREETS
Has It Come To This?

6 DIZZEE RASCAL
I Luv U

7 ROBIN S
Show Me Love

8 SISQO
Thong Song (Artful Dodger Remix)

DRUM 'N' BASS

Rock The Funky Beat...

1 **SHY FX**
Shake Ur Body

2 **Q PROJECT**
Champion Sound

3 **FOUL PLAY**
Renegade Snares (Remix)

4 **GOLDIE PRESENTS METALHEADS**
Inner City Life

5 **SHIMON & ANDY C**
Bodyrock

6 **DJ HYPE**
Super Sharp Shooter

7 **DJ ZINC**
Reach Out (Remix)

8 **DILLINJA**
Grimey

WORLD MUSIC

Cruel Crazy Beautiful World...

1 **NUSRAT FATEH ALI KHAN**
Musst Musst

2 **PABLO 'LUBADIKA' PORTHOS**
Madeleine

3 **BALFA BROTHERS**
Tit Galop Pour Mamou

4 **OS MUTANTES**
A Minha Menina

5 **LADYSMITH BLACK MAMBAZO**
Swing Low Sweet Chariot

6 **PAUL SIMON**
Diamonds On The Soles Of Her Shoes

7 **OFRA HAZA**
Im Nin'Alu

8 **THE BHUNDU BOYS**
Manhenga

GENERAL INDEX

INDEX OF ARTISTS

INDEX OF SONGS